LEVEL 1

George Washington Carver

Kitson Jazynka

NATIONAL GEOGRAPHIC

Washington, D.C.

For kids who love to discover, learn, and teach, like George Washington Carver did —K. J.

Copyright © 2016 National Geographic Society

Published by National Geographic Partners, LLC, Washington, D.C. 20036. All rights reserved. Reproduction in whole or in part without written permission of the publisher is prohibited.

NATIONAL GEOGRAPHIC and Yellow Border Design are trademarks of the National Geographic Society, used under license.

Trade paperback ISBN: 978-1-4263-2285-3
Reinforced library binding ISBN: 978-1-4263-2286-0

Editor: Shelby Alinsky
Art Director: Callie Broaddus
Editorial: Snapdragon Books
Designer: YAY! Design
Photo Editor: Christina Ascani
Special Projects Assistant: Kathryn Williams
Rights Clearance Specialists: Michael Cassady & Mari Robinson
Design Production Assistants: Sanjida Rashid & Rachel Kenny
Manufacturing Manager: Rachel Faulise
Production Editor: Mike O'Connor
Managing Editor: Grace Hill

The publisher and author gratefully acknowledge the expert content review of this book by Paxton J. Williams, Esq., former executive director of the George Washington Carver Birthplace Association, and the literacy review of this book by Mariam Jean Dreher, professor of reading education at the University of Maryland, College Park.

National Geographic supports K–12 educators with ELA Common Core Resources.
Visit natgeoed.org/commoncore for more information.

Collection copyright © 2018 National Geographic Partners, LLC
Collection ISBN (paperback): 978-1-4263-3201-2
Collection ISBN (library edition): 978-1-4263-3202-9

Printed in the United States of America
18/WOR/1

Table of Contents

Who Was Carver?

George Washington Carver loved studying plants. He showed farmers how to grow sustainable (suh-STANE-uh-bul) crops. That helped them farm better and eat better.

He also found that hundreds of things could be made from peanut plants. Growing peanuts helped farmers earn money.

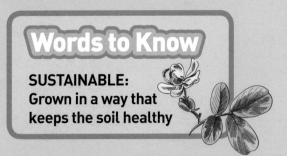

Words to Know

SUSTAINABLE: Grown in a way that keeps the soil healthy

This painting of George Washington Carver was made in 1942.

Many black farmers were too poor to buy their own land. Instead, they had to rent it. They paid the owner a share of their crops.

In Carver's time, life was hard for many black people in the United States. They did not have the same rights as white people.

Carver felt that this was wrong. He used his ideas about farming to help change people's lives.

Carver was one of the most famous African Americans of his time.

Growing Up

The cabin where Carver lived as a boy is gone. This outline (photo above) was built later to show how small it was. This sketch (right) was drawn by Carver. It shows how he remembers the cabin.

George Washington Carver was born on a farm near Diamond, Missouri, U.S.A.

Most people think he was born around 1864. No one knows for sure. But we do know he was born a slave.

Back then, slaves were often given their owner's last name. George's owners were Moses and Susan Carver. So his last name was Carver too.

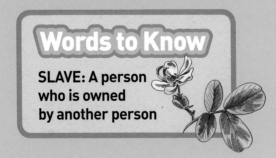

Words to Know

SLAVE: A person who is owned by another person

This statue shows Carver as a boy. It stands at the George Washington Carver National Monument in Diamond, Missouri. This was the first national monument to honor an African American.

One night, men kidnapped baby George Carver and his mother. He was returned to the farm, but his mother was not.

Soon after, slavery ended. Moses and Susan Carver decided to raise George. As a boy, he loved to explore the farm. He collected rocks. He grew a garden. He asked questions.

In His Own Words

"When I talk to the little flower or to the little peanut, they will give up their secrets."

In His Time

Carver grew up in the midwestern United States during the 1870s. Back then, many things were different from how they are today.

TRANSPORTATION: Many people traveled on foot, in wagons pulled by horses, or by steamboat or train.

MONEY: Most freed slaves had little or no money. They often traded for things they needed.

FOOD: Few people shopped in stores for food. Instead, they raised farm animals. They also grew fruits and vegetables to feed their families.

SCHOOL: Children went to school in one-room schoolhouses or even old barns.

U.S. EVENTS: In 1872, Ulysses S. Grant was re-elected president of the United States.

TOYS AND FUN: Children spent time outdoors and played with handmade toys.

A Love of Learning

Carver loved to learn. But in his town, black children could not go to school. Carver learned to read at home. He had only one book.

In His Own Words

"My soul thirsted for an education."

This drawing shows a school for black children during Carver's time.

Carver wanted to learn more.
At around age 13, he left home.
He lived with a black family
in a nearby town. There he went
to a school for black children.

Later, Carver wanted to go to college. Many black Americans still faced racism (RAY-siz-um). One school would not let Carver in because he was black.

But he didn't give up. He became the first black student at Iowa State College. He studied agriculture (AG-ri-kul-chur).

Words to Know

RACISM: The belief that one group of people is better than another

AGRICULTURE: The science of farming

In 1894, Carver got his degree from Iowa State College (shown below).

6 COOL FACTS About Carver

1 Carver grew up on a farm with horses, cattle, honeybees, and wheat crops.

2 As a boy, Carver helped people with their sick plants. They called him the "plant doctor."

3 The U.S. Navy named two ships after Carver.

Carver added "Washington" to his name because another George Carver lived in his town.

Carver loved art. He made paint from berries. He tied twigs together for a brush.

Three U.S. presidents asked for Carver's advice on farming.

Carver meeting President Franklin D. Roosevelt in 1939

Helping Others

After college, Carver became a teacher. He worked at a school in Alabama called Tuskegee Institute (tuh-SKEE-gee IN-stuh-toot).

Carver (front row, center) sits with his fellow teachers at Tuskegee Institute.

Carver (second from right) taught in this lab at Tuskegee Institute in 1906.

There he did important work with plants. He found many new ways to use sweet potatoes and soybeans. He invented hundreds of new things, such as paints, plastics, and dyes.

He also wanted to help farmers. He built a classroom on a wagon. It was pulled by mules. He drove the wagon to nearby farms to teach about agriculture.

This was the first wagon classroom Carver used.

Most farmers couldn't come to Carver's classroom. So Carver wanted to bring his ideas to them.

Carver thought that planting peanuts could help farmers too. Peanut plants would keep the soil healthy.

Carver said a massage with peanut oil could help a sick person. The oil was sold in bottles like these.

Farmers could also sell this crop to earn more money. Carver had found more than 300 ways to use peanut plants. They could be turned into glue, medicine, gasoline, and even paper.

Good Ideas

Carver traveled. He gave speeches about farming. He spoke about peanuts. He also spoke about treating all people fairly.

In 1921, he spoke to the U.S. Congress. Some people in Congress didn't want to listen to a black man. But he had good ideas. Finally Congress listened. They shared his ideas with others.

1864
Born around this year

1865
Slavery ends in the United States

1877
Leaves home to go to school

In His Own Words

"I want to feel that my life has been of some service to my fellow man."

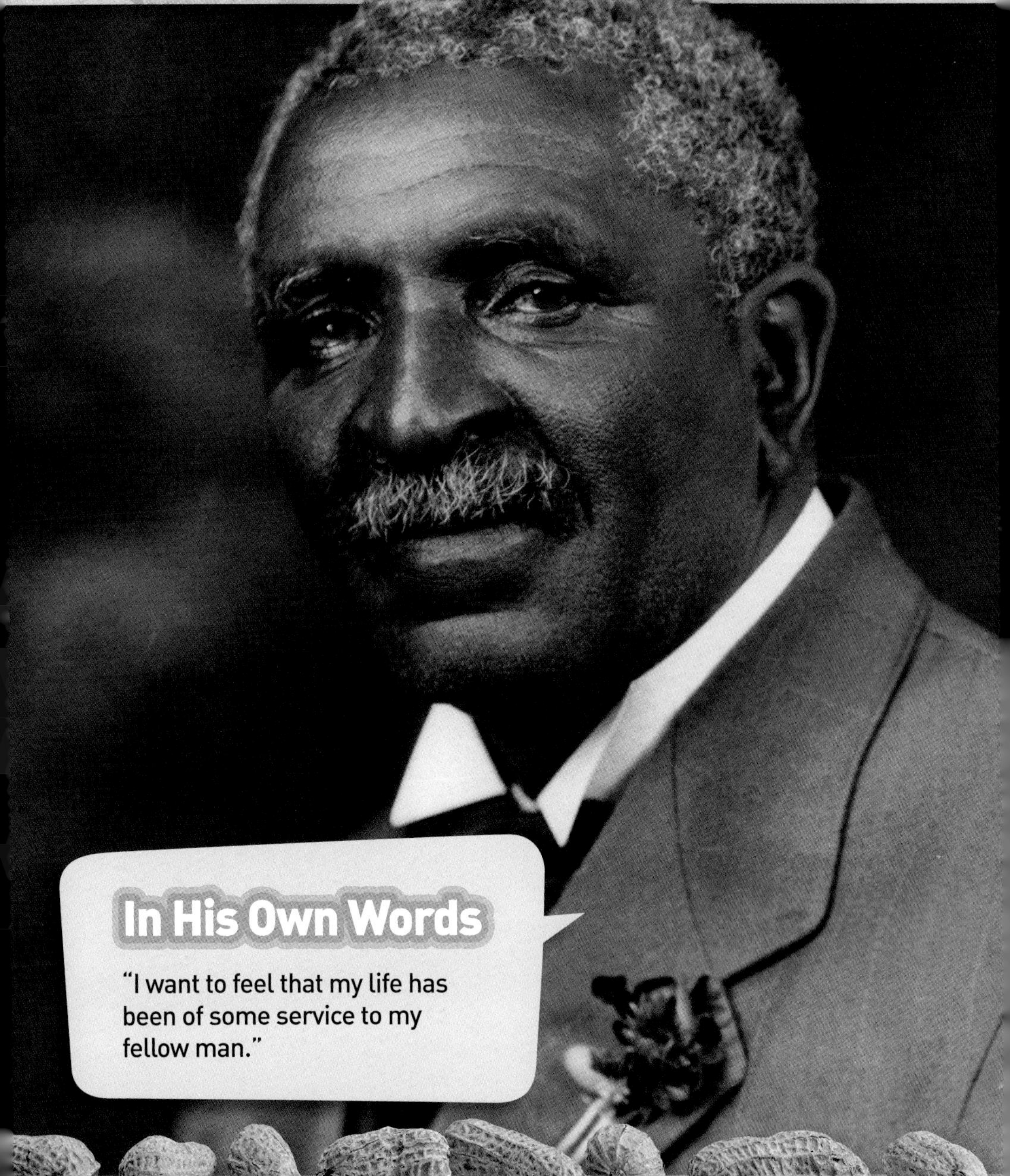

1894

Earns his first degree from Iowa State College

1896

Earns another degree from Iowa State College

Hard Work

Carver died in 1943. He was around 79 years old. Carver's hard work helped many people. His ideas helped poor farmers have better lives. His story shows the power of learning and helping others.

GEORGE WASHINGTON CARVER

1896

Starts teaching at Tuskegee Institute in Alabama

1921

Speaks to U.S. Congress about the many uses of peanuts

The George Washington Carver Museum at Tuskegee Institute

Carver's picture appeared on a 32-cent U.S. postage stamp in 1998. It was the second stamp with his picture.

32 USA

George Washington Carver

1998

1943

Dies on January 5

1948

His picture appears on a three-cent U.S. postage stamp

1965

The U.S. Navy names a submarine the U.S.S. *George Washington Carver*

What in the World?

These pictures show up-close views of items from George Washington Carver's time. Use the hints to figure out what's in the pictures. Answers are on page 31.

1

HINT: Carver found many uses for this crop.

2

HINT: The U.S. Navy named two of these in Carver's honor.

Word Bank

mules   berries   books   rocks   ships   peanuts

3

HINT: Carver loved to read but had only one of these as a child.

4

HINT: These animals pulled Carver's wagon classroom.

5

HINT: Carver made paint with these.

6

HINT: Carver collected these on the farm where he grew up.

Answers: 1. peanuts, 2. ships, 3. books, 4. mules, 5. berries, 6. rocks

AGRICULTURE: The science of farming

RACISM: The belief that one group of people is better than another

SLAVE: A person who is owned by another person

SUSTAINABLE: Grown in a way that keeps the soil healthy

LEVEL
2

Rosa Parks

Kitson Jazynka

NATIONAL
GEOGRAPHIC

Washington, D.C.

To all the kids who stand up for what's right. —K. J.

Trade paperback ISBN: 978-1-4263-2141-2
Reinforced library binding ISBN:
978-1-4263-2142-9

Editor: Shelby Alinsky
Art Director: Callie Broaddus
Editorial: Snapdragon Books
Designer: YAY! Design
Photo Editor: Lori Epstein
Production Assistants: Sanjida Rashid and Rachel Kenny
Rights Clearance Specialist: Michael Cassady
Manufacturing Manager: Rachel Faulise

The author and publisher gratefully acknowledge the expert content review of this book by Charles M. Payne, Ph.D., School of Social Service Administration, University of Chicago, and the literacy review of this book by Mariam Jean Dreher, professor of reading education, University of Maryland, College Park.

The publisher gratefully acknowledges the Rosa & Raymond Parks Institute for Self Development for their assistance in licensing the photos of Rosa Parks and in reviewing the contents and accuracy of this book.

Photo Credits

**National Geographic supports K–12 educators with ELA Common Core Resources.
Visit natgeoed.org/commoncore for more information.**

Table of Contents

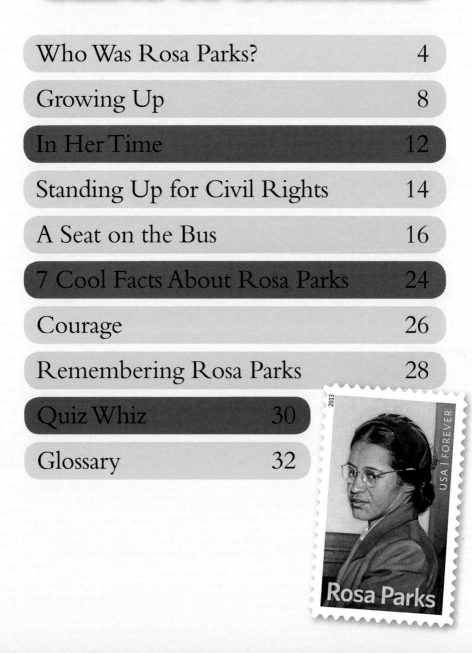

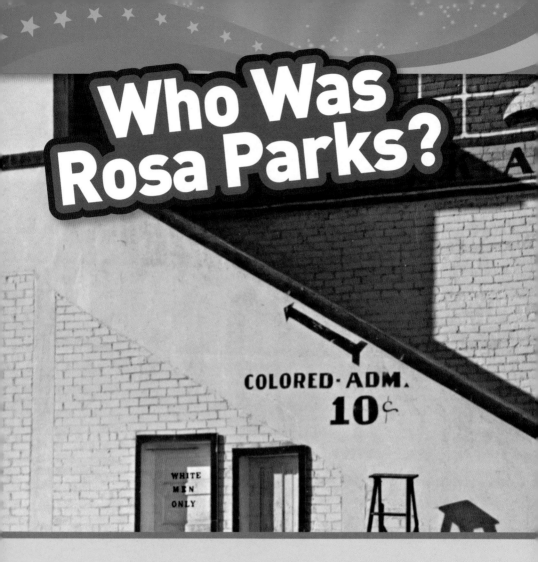

Who Was Rosa Parks?

COLORED·ADM.
10¢

WHITE
MEN
ONLY

Can you imagine a world where
white children could ride a school
bus every morning, but black children
had to walk? Can you imagine a
world where black people couldn't

There was a time when black people had to use separate back entrances to movie theaters and restaurants.

drink from the same water fountains as white people or sit with them on a city bus?

This world was real. And it happened in the United States.

For COLORED ONLY

Some white people felt they should be treated better than black people. Segregation (SEG-rih-GAY-shun) laws were used to give more rights and a better life to white people.

Word to Know

SEGREGATION: the act of keeping a group apart from others

Rosa Parks helped change these unfair laws by thinking and acting. She stood up for herself and others her whole life.

In Her Own Words

"If I did not resist being mistreated . . . I would spend the rest of my life being mistreated."

Growing Up

Rosa Parks was born as Rosa Louise McCauley on February 4, 1913, in Tuskegee, Alabama.

She lived on a farm with her parents and grandparents. She was a small, quiet girl. She loved to read nursery rhymes and fairy tales like "Little Red Riding Hood." She also helped take care of her little brother, Sylvester.

an early portrait of Rosa

Nov. 1956

Rosa's grandparents were born as slaves. They taught her that all people deserve fair treatment. When Rosa was a child, slavery was over. But white people still had more freedom than black people.

Like the people pictured here, all black Americans were free in the 1920s. However, unfair laws made their lives difficult.

To help her parents pay for school after sixth grade, Rosa cleaned classrooms in the afternoon.

When she was 11 years old, Rosa moved to Montgomery, Alabama, to attend this school, the Montgomery Industrial School for Girls.

One day when Rosa was 11, a white boy pushed her. She pushed back. The boy's mother told Rosa she would go to jail. Rosa stood up for herself. She told them she didn't want to be pushed.

In Her Time

When Rosa was a girl in the 1920s, many things were different from how they are today.

TRANSPORTATION: White people and black people paid the same price to ride the bus, but they didn't have the same rules. White people could sit up front, but black people had to sit in the back.

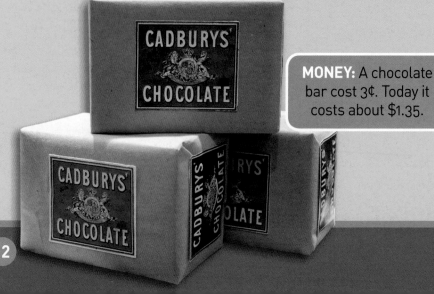

MONEY: A chocolate bar cost 3¢. Today it costs about $1.35.

U.S. EVENTS: In 1920, women were allowed to vote for the first time in U.S. history.

TOYS AND FUN: Children played games like marbles and kick the can, which is similar to hide-and-seek.

SCHOOL: Many black children in the southern United States went to school only six months a year because they had to work in the fields to help their families. For the same reason, most black children didn't go to school past the sixth grade.

Standing Up for Civil Rights

When Rosa was 19 years old, she married Raymond Parks. They lived in Montgomery. She got a job as a seamstress in a department store. She sewed clothes to fit customers.

Like the people in this photo, Rosa Parks helped black people sign up to vote. There were many challenges. Parks herself tried three times before she was allowed to sign up to vote.

Rosa Parks also worked to spread the word about

civil rights. She attended meetings, rallies, and marches. She taught young people how to stand up for themselves. She helped people who were hurt by those who did not believe in civil rights. Standing up for civil rights was not easy. But Parks never gave up.

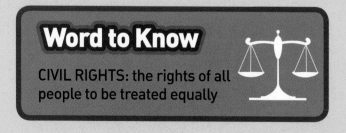

Word to Know

CIVIL RIGHTS: the rights of all people to be treated equally

A Seat on the Bus

On the night of December 1, 1955, Parks took the bus home after work. She sat down in a seat in the middle of the bus.

Parks riding a bus in Montgomery

After a few stops, the bus grew crowded. The driver asked Parks to stand so a white man could sit. She thought about the unfairness she'd faced all her life. She felt she had as much right to sit in the seat as anyone else, no matter the color of her skin.

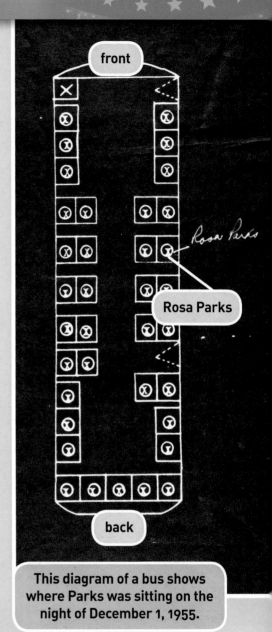

front

Rosa Parks

Rosa Parks

back

This diagram of a bus shows where Parks was sitting on the night of December 1, 1955.

Parks looked the driver in the eye. In a quiet voice she answered, "No."

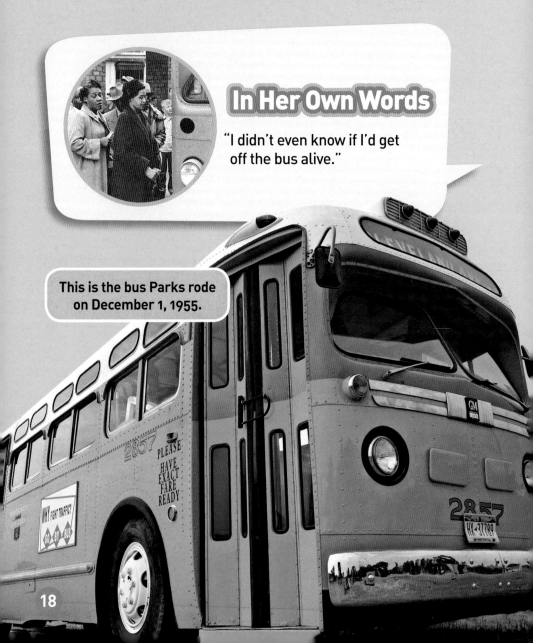

In Her Own Words

"I didn't even know if I'd get off the bus alive."

This is the bus Parks rode on December 1, 1955.

PLEASE HAVE EXACT FARE READY

2857

black and white passengers on a city bus

She must have been scared. Black people had been arrested for refusing to give up a seat on a bus. Some had even been hurt or killed for doing the same thing. People on the bus—black and white—feared what would happen.

The bus driver called the police. The police arrested Parks. At her trial, the court found her guilty of breaking a state segregation law. She was forced to pay a fine.

In Her Own Words

"People always say that I didn't give up my seat because I was tired, but that isn't true . . . No, the only tired I was, was tired of giving in."

Name **Parks**
　　　　　Surname
Alias
Nickname:
No. **79521** Co

I. Thumb

Parks faced the police many times as she fought for civil rights. This photo is from one such arrest.

That's a FACT!

When the police officer told Parks he was going to arrest her on the bus that day, she replied, "You may do that."

Word spread about what had happened. Parks's act inspired people to stand up for fair and equal treatment.

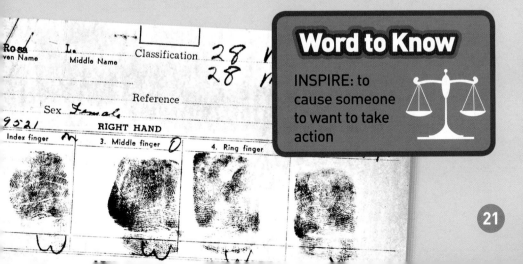

Ro sa   L.
Given Name   Middle Name

Classification 28
              28

Reference

Sex Female

9521

RIGHT HAND

Index finger   3. Middle finger   4. Ring finger

Word to Know

INSPIRE: to cause someone to want to take action

Black leaders asked people to protest unfair rules by taking part in a bus boycott. A young preacher named Martin Luther King, Jr., made a speech. He urged people to stick together.

Words to Know

PROTEST: to say you don't agree with something

BOYCOTT: the act of refusing to use a service as a way to protest it

It was not easy for people to get to work and other places without the bus. But people kept the boycott going. It lasted more than a year. Finally, the Supreme Court ruled that everyone had the same rights on buses.

People boycotting the buses wave to an empty bus driving by.

7 COOL FACTS
About Rosa Parks

IF YOU NEED A RIDE Come To: Anderson's Chapel At: 816 Page Ave. Anytime Between 6:00 A.M. + 6:00 P.M. REMEMBER!!!

1

Parks was not the first black person to refuse to give up a seat on a bus, but her actions sparked the famous bus boycott that helped change unfair laws.

2

Parks was part Native American.

3

In Montgomery, Alabama, you can visit the bus stop where police arrested Parks.

In 2012, President Barack Obama sat on the bus Parks was riding when she refused to give up her seat. The bus is on display at the Henry Ford Museum in Detroit, Michigan.

Today a statue of Parks stands in the U.S. Capitol Building in Washington, D.C.

When Parks died in 2005, bus drivers in Montgomery and Detroit honored her by reserving their front seats.

Many people call Parks the Mother of the Civil Rights Movement.

Courage

Parks paid a price for protesting. After her arrest, Parks and her husband lost their jobs. Angry people threatened them. Finally, in 1957, they left Montgomery and moved to Detroit.

In 1965, Parks took a job with a black congressman named John Conyers. For the next 20 years, she worked in Conyers's office.

1913
Born on February 4 in Tuskegee, Alabama

1924
Moves to Montgomery, Alabama, to continue school

1932
Marries Raymond Parks

Parks continued to stand up for civil rights. She attended meetings and peaceful protests. She even helped black people fight unfairness in other countries, like South Africa.

Parks protesting South Africa's unfair laws

FREEDOM YES APARTHEID NO

Word to Know

PEACEFUL: without fighting or arguing

1955

Refuses to give up her seat on a bus and sparks a famous boycott

1956

U.S. Supreme Court rules that segregation on buses is unlawful

1957

Moves with her husband to Detroit, Michigan

Remembering Rosa Parks

Many people know about Parks's life because she refused to give up her seat on the bus that day in 1955. But now you know she spent her whole life standing up for fair treatment.

That's a FACT! In 1996, President Bill Clinton awarded Parks the Presidential Medal of Freedom.

1965

Takes a job with Congressman John Conyers

1996

Awarded the Presidential Medal of Freedom at the White House

1999

Named one of the top 20 most important people of the century by *Time* magazine

Rosa Parks died on October 24, 2005, at age 92. After her death, she was given great honors, like the ones presidents and soldiers receive.

2005

Dies on October 24, at age 92

2006

Remembered with a statue in the U.S. Capitol Building in Washington, D.C.

2013

U.S. Postal Service creates a stamp in Parks's honor on what would have been her 100th birthday

QUIZ WHIZ

See how many questions you can get right!
Answers are at the bottom of page 31.

1

Segregation laws . . .

A. made sure kids went to school.
B. made sure all people could vote.
C. kept black people and
   white people apart.
D. kept people from driving too fast.

2

Where was Parks born?

A. Alabama
B. Michigan
C. Washington, D.C.
D. South Africa

Parks's grandparents . . .

A. died before she was born.
B. were born as slaves.
C. lived in a mansion.
D. owned a department store.

3

4

Parks stood up for civil rights by . . .

A. helping black people sign up to vote.
B. attending meetings, rallies, and marches.
C. teaching young people how to stand up for themselves.
D. doing all of the above.

What did Parks do when the bus driver asked her to stand?

A. She gave up her seat and stood.
B. She stayed in her seat to protest.
C. She got off the bus and walked.
D. She tied herself to the seat.

5

6

What happened during the bus boycott?

A. The bus ran out of gas.
B. People rode the bus for free.
C. Buses did not run.
D. People did not ride buses.

Why did Parks and her husband move to Detroit?

A. They wanted to retire.
B. She needed to care for her mother.
C. She wanted to return to her hometown.
D. They lost their jobs and were threatened.

7

BOYCOTT: the act of refusing to use a service as a way to protest it

CIVIL RIGHTS: the rights of all people to be treated equally

INSPIRE: to cause someone to want to take action

PEACEFUL: without fighting or arguing

PROTEST: to say you don't agree with something

SEGREGATION: the act of keeping a group apart from others

Frederick Douglass

Barbara Kramer

NATIONAL
GEOGRAPHIC

Washington, D.C.

To my writers' group—Karry, Barb, and Barb
—B. K.

Library of Congress Cataloging-in-Publication Data

Names: Kramer, Barbara, author.
Title: Frederick Douglass / Barbara Kramer.
Description: Washington, DC : National Geographic, 2017. | Series: National Geographic readers
Identifiers: LCCN 2016038837 (print) | LCCN 2016040010 (ebook) | ISBN 9781426327568 (pbk. : alk. paper) | ISBN 9781426327575 (hardcover : alk. paper) | ISBN 9781426327582 (e-book)
Subjects: LCSH: Douglass, Frederick, 1818-1895—Juvenile literature. | African American abolitionists—Biography—Juvenile literature. | Slaves—United States—Biography—Juvenile literature. | Slavery—United States—History—Juvenile literature.
Classification: LCC E449.D75 K73 2017 (print) | LCC E449.D75 (ebook) | DDC 973.8092 [B] —dc23

LC record available at lccn.loc.gov/2016038837

The publisher and author gratefully acknowledge the expert content review of this book by Robert S. Levine, Ph.D., Department of English, University of Maryland, and author of several titles on Frederick Douglass, including The Lives of Frederick Douglass (2015), and the literacy review of this book by Mariam Jean Dreher, professor of reading education, University of Maryland, College Park.

Photo Credits
Cover: (LO), Bettmann/Getty Images; (background), Brandon Seidel/Shutterstock; 1, MPI/Getty Images; 3, Universal Images Group North America LLC/Alamy Stock Photo; 4, Granger.com—All rights reserved; 6, Granger.com—All rights reserved; 7, Highsmith, Carol M, Library of Congress Prints and Photographs Division; 8-9, Bennett, W. J., Library of Congress Prints and Photographs Division; 9 (CTR), North Wind Picture Archives/Alamy Stock Photo; 10, Granger.com—All rights reserved; 11 (UP), The New York Public Library, Schomburg Center For Research In Black Culture, Manuscripts, Archives And Rare Books Division; 11 (CTR), Bettmann/Getty Images; 11 (LO LE), Library of Congress/Getty Images; 13-15, Granger.com—All rights reserved; 17, Granger.com—All rights reserved; 18, Universal History Archive/Getty Images; 19, Newberry Library, Chicago, Illinois, USA/Bridgeman Images; 20, North Wind Picture Archives/Alamy Stock Photo; 21, Science & Society Picture Library/Getty Images; 22 (UP), Nuilko/Getty Images; 22 (CTR), Highsmith, Carol M., Library of Congress Prints and Photographs Division; 22 (LO), Clarke Conde/Alamy Stock Photo; 23 (UP), Universal History Archive/Getty Images; 23 (CTR), Collection of the Smithsonian National Museum of African American History and Culture, Gift of Elizabeth Cassell; 23 (LO), pf/Alamy Stock Photo; 24, Library of Congress Prints and Photographs Division; 25 (UP LE), National Park Service; 25 (UP RT), Courtesy of the Moorland-Spingarn Research Center, Howard University, Washington DC; 26 (CTR), Bettmann/Getty Images; 26-27 (LO), Flas100/Shutterstock; 27 (UP), Niday Picture Library/Alamy Stock Photo; 28 (CTR), National Park Service; 28-29 (LO), Flas100/Shutterstock; 29 (UP), North Wind Picture Archives/Alamy Stock Photo; 29 (CTR), Drew Angerer/Getty Images; 30 (UP), North Wind Picture Archives/Alamy Stock Photo; 30 (CTR), Granger.com—All rights reserved; 30 (LO), Universal History Archive/Getty Images; 31 (UP), Granger.com—All rights reserved; 31 (UP CTR & CTR CTR), alexsl/Getty Images; 31 (LO CTR), Poligrafistka/Getty Images; 31 (CTR RT), charnsitr/Shutterstock; 31 (CTR & LO), Hulton Archive/Getty Images; 32 (UP LE), Pictorial Press Ltd/Alamy Stock Photo; 32 (UP RT), MPI/Getty Images; 32 (CTR LE), NG Maps; 32 (CTR RT), North Wind Picture Archives/Alamy Stock Photo; 32 (LO LE), Granger.com—All rights reserved; 32 (LO RT), Bettmann/Getty Images; header, Library of Congress Prints and Photographs Divisionvocab, The Washington Post/Getty Images

National Geographic supports K–12 educators with ELA Common Core Resources. Visit natgeoed.org/commoncore for more information.

Table of Contents

Who Was Frederick Douglass?

a painting of
Frederick Douglass,
from around 1844

Frederick Douglass was born a slave. He worked hard for his master for no money. His master told Douglass where to live, what to eat, and what to do.

After 20 years as a slave, Douglass escaped. He began speaking out against slavery. He didn't stop until all slaves were free. Then he worked to help freed slaves have better lives.

Words to Know

MASTER: A person who owns slaves

SLAVERY: The practice of owning slaves

Born a Slave

Douglass was born in February 1818 on a farm in Talbot County, Maryland, U.S.A. Soon after his birth, his mother was sent to work on another farm. Douglass only saw her four or five times. She died when he was seven. He never knew his father.

a wood engraving of slaves working with cotton in the American South

Douglass's grandfather was a free man, but his grandmother was a slave. She took care of slaves who were too young to work.

As an adult, Douglass had this cabin built in his backyard in Washington, D.C. It looked like the one where he had lived with his grandparents.

Douglass spent his early years with his grandparents. They lived in a cabin about 12 miles from his master's farm.

When Douglass was about six years old, his grandmother took him to their master's farm. She didn't want to leave him there, but she had to do what their owner said. Douglass knew then that he was expected to obey the master, too.

About two years later, Douglass was sent to Baltimore, Maryland, to work. He had heard stories about that city and was excited to go.

In His Own Words

"I didn't know I was a slave until I found out I couldn't do the things I wanted."

Baltimore Harbor in 1831, during the time Douglass lived there

In His Time

In the 1820s, growing up as a slave was very different from growing up as a child who was free.

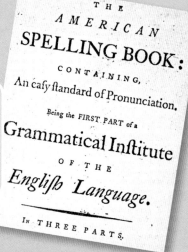

THE
AMERICAN
SPELLING BOOK:
CONTAINING,
An eafy ftandard of Pronunciation.
Being the FIRST PART of a
Grammatical Inftitute
OF THE
Englifh Language.

In THREE PARTS.

SCHOOL: Slaves did not attend school. Teaching a slave to read was against the law in some states. An education would give a slave power.

EVENTS: Some people helped slaves escape from their masters. The group of people who led slaves to safety was called the Underground Railroad.

Please to let Benjamin McDaniel pass to Dr. Henkal's in New-Market, Shenandoah County, Va. or Tuesday to Montpelier, for Mr. Madison and return on Monday.

June 1st 1843.

TRAVEL: Slaves who traveled without their owners had to carry a pass from their masters. Black people who were free had to carry papers saying they were not slaves.

RIGHTS: Slaves had no rights. Slaves were listed as property along with the slave owner's animals. They could be sold to other slave owners at any time, often separating children from their parents.

FREEDOM: When their masters died, a few slaves were given their freedom. But most got new owners, so they were still not free. Sometimes slaves could buy their freedom. But since most slaves did not earn money for their work, that rarely happened.

Words to Know

FREEDOM: The power to move or act as you wish and do what you want to do

Learning to Read

In Baltimore, Douglass worked
for Hugh Auld (HUE ALLD)
and his wife. He took care of
their young son and ran errands.
Mrs. Auld started teaching Douglass
to read. Mr. Auld told her to stop.
He said slaves should know only one
thing—how to obey their master.

But Douglass kept learning. He gave
biscuits (BISS-kits) to poor white
children he met on his errands.
In return, they helped him read.

This wood engraving shows Mrs. Auld teaching Douglass to read.

That's a FACT! With 50 cents Douglass earned from polishing shoes, he bought a book of famous speeches and read it many times.

When Douglass was 15, he was sent back to the farm. His master had died. He now had a new owner. Douglass had to work hard in the field. He was often treated badly. He tried to escape, but he was caught.

Slaves often worked long hours in the fields. They worked on a large farm or group of farms called a plantation.

Other slave owners were angry. Douglass had set a bad example for their slaves. To avoid trouble, Douglass's new master sent Douglass back to Baltimore to work for the Auld family again.

That's a FACT! When Douglass was working as a field slave, he held secret classes to teach other slaves to read.

Runaway Slave

In Baltimore, Douglass met free black people. He fell in love with a free black woman named Anna Murray. More than ever, he wanted to be free.

On September 3, 1838, he tried to escape again. He headed north by boat and train. If he were caught, he might be killed or sold. But he made it to New York, a free state. He sent for Anna, and they got married.

Words to Know

FREE STATE: A U.S. state that did not allow people to own slaves

16

That's a FACT! Over time, Douglass and Anna had five children: three boys and two girls.

an illustration of Douglass and his wife, Anna, soon after they were married

Douglass had escaped, but he was still a slave. Soon he became well known for his speeches and his book. That put him in danger. Now it was easier for his master to find him. Douglass had to get away. But it meant leaving his family behind.

Many people wanted to hear Douglass speak. He talked about the abolition of slavery, which is the act of ending slavery.

an illustration of a steamship similar to the one on which Douglass traveled to England

He sailed to England. He gave speeches there and made many friends. They raised money to buy his freedom. At last, Douglass was free!

6 COOL FACTS About Douglass

1 As a young man in Baltimore, Douglass learned to play the violin. It was a hobby he enjoyed the rest of his life.

2 Douglass met with President Abraham Lincoln three times during the Civil War. After the president died, Mrs. Lincoln gave her husband's favorite walking stick to Douglass.

FREDERICK DOUGLASS HOME SITE

Frederick Douglass

Who Lived Here?

3 Douglass became active in the Underground Railroad. His home in Rochester, New York, was a stopping place. Runaway slaves could hide there until it was safe to travel to the next stop. Today, people can visit there.

4

Douglass was known as a great storyteller. He often made family, friends, and audiences laugh with his tales.

Douglass wrote three books about his life: *Narrative of the Life of Frederick Douglass*, *My Bondage and My Freedom*, and *Life and Times of Frederick Douglass*.

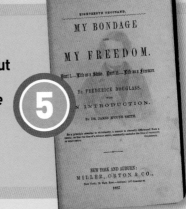

5

6

In 1899, four years after Douglass died, a statue of him was built in Rochester, New York. It was the first time an African American was honored with a statue.

A Fight to End Slavery

In 1847, Douglass returned to the United States. He moved his family to Rochester, New York. There he started a newspaper called the *North Star*. He wrote articles against slavery for the paper.

Sam¹ Brooke

THE NORTH STAR.

RIGHT IS OF NO SEX—TRUTH IS OF NO COLOR—GOD IS THE FATHER OF US ALL, AND ALL WE ARE BRETHREN.

ROCHESTER, N. Y., FRIDAY, JUNE 2, 1848.

VOL. 1. NO. 23.   WHOLE NO.—23.

When slaves tried to escape, they looked up to the sky and followed the North Star. This is how the paper got its name.

Charles Douglass

Lewis Douglass

That's a FACT! Two of Douglass's sons were among the first African Americans to sign up to fight in the Civil War.

People in the United States did not agree about slavery. That led to the start of the Civil War in 1861. Douglass organized a group of African Americans to fight in that war.

Words to Know

CIVIL WAR: A war between different groups of people from the same country

New Beginnings

The Civil War led to the end of slavery. But black people were still not treated the same as white people. Douglass gave speeches about treating all people the same.

In His Own Words

"I would unite with anybody to do right and with nobody to do wrong."

1818
Born in February

1824
Sent to live on his master's farm

1826
Begins work as a house slave in Baltimore

Douglass also gave speeches about allowing women to vote.

Douglass with Helen Pitts

In 1882, Anna got sick and died. Douglass was sad and lonely. About two years later, he married Helen Pitts. That upset many people because Helen was white.

1838
Escapes from slavery; marries Anna Murray

1841
Gives his first speech against slavery

Douglass never stopped speaking out to help others. On February 20, 1895, he gave a speech to a women's group. He died at home later that day. He was 77 years old.

Douglass at work in the library at Cedar Hill, his home in Washington, D.C.

1845

Publishes the first of three books about his life

1846

Friends in England buy his freedom

"Abolition of slavery had been the deepest desire and the great labor of my life."

Douglass was a powerful voice for those who believe that all people should be treated equally. Today, his words still inspire others all over the world.

a statue of Douglass in the United States Capitol Building in Washington, D.C.

1847
Starts his newspaper, the *North Star*

1884
Marries Helen Pitts

1895
Dies on February 20

QUIZ WHIZ

See how many questions you can get right!
Answers are at the bottom of page 31.

1

Who took care of Douglass until he was about six years old?

A. his master's wife
B. his mother
C. his aunt
D. his grandmother

2

The first person to help Douglass learn to read was

_____.

A. a white friend
B. his grandmother
C. Mrs. Auld
D. another slave

How old was Douglass when he was sent back to the farm after living in Baltimore?

A. 12
B. 15
C. 18
D. 20

3

4

Douglas was still a slave when he escaped Baltimore to go to New York.

A. true
B. false

Douglass traveled to what country to keep from being caught and returned to his master?

A. Senegal
B. Canada
C. England
D. Mexico

5

6

Douglass started a newspaper called _____.

A. the *Underground Railroad*
B. the *North Star*
C. the *Slave Papers*
D. the *Life and Times of Frederick Douglass*

Which one of these statements about slavery is true?

A. Slaves could travel where they wanted.
B. Young slaves were taught to read.
C. Slaves who escaped to free states were safe.
D. Slaves had to obey their masters.

7

ABOLISH: To officially stop something, such as a law

CIVIL WAR: A war between different groups of people from the same country

Free state, 1861

Slave state, 1861

Border state, 1861

U.S. territory, 1861

FREE STATE: A U.S. state that did not allow people to own slaves

FREEDOM: The power to move or act as you wish and do what you want to do

MASTER: A person who owns slaves

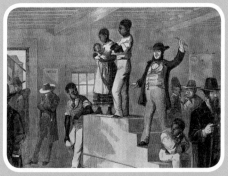

SLAVERY: The practice of owning slaves

LEVEL

3

Martin Luther King, Jr.

Kitson Jazynka

NATIONAL
GEOGRAPHIC

Washington, D.C.

To bright young readers everywhere,
especially Max & Quinn —K. J.

The publisher and author gratefully acknowledge the review of proofs for this book by historian
Michael K. Honey.

Library of Congress Cataloging-in-Publication Data
Jazynka, Kitson.
Martin Luther King, Jr. / by Kitson Jazynka.
p. cm. Includes index.
ISBN 978-1-4263-1087-4 (pbk. : alk. paper) -- ISBN 978-1-4263-1088-1 (library binding : alk. paper) 1. King, Martin Luther, Jr.,
1929-1968--Juvenile literature. 2. African Americans--Biography--Juvenile literature. 3. Civil rights workers--United States--
Biography--Juvenile literature. 4. Baptists--United States--Clergy--Biography--Juvenile literature.
5. African Americans--Civil rights--History--20th century--Juvenile literature. I. Title.
E185.97.K5J377 2012
323.092--dc23
[B]
2012034595

National Geographic supports K–12 educators with ELA Common Core Resources.
Visit natgeoed.org/commoncore for more information.

Table of Contents

Who Was Martin Luther King, Jr.?

Can you imagine a world where laws kept black and white people apart? Where black children couldn't swim in the same pools as white children? Or go to the same schools? A place where laws made it hard for black people to vote? Or where a black person had to stand up on a bus so a white person could sit down?

This world was real. And it happened in the United States.

Words to Know

CIVIL RIGHTS: The rights that all people in the U.S. have to be treated as equals

Statues at the National Civil Rights Museum in Memphis, Tennessee

Martin Luther King, Jr., worked hard to change rules so they would be the same for whites and blacks. He didn't do it by fighting. He helped change unfair laws by making people think. He did it by making people feel. He did it with his words.

Words to Know

PROTEST: To say you don't agree with something

Protesters

People who protest are called protesters. When protesters want unfair things changed, they sometimes march to show others that they do not agree with what is happening.

Dr. King marches in a protest.

Lots of black people and white people helped Dr. King protest those laws. This made many people angry because they didn't want change. But in the end, the protesters won. And the rules changed forever.

Growing Up

Dr. King was born in 1929 in Atlanta, Georgia. He was named after his father. He was called M.L.

Small but strong, M.L. rode bikes with his brother and sister.

That's a Fact!

M.L.'s boyhood home on Auburn Avenue in Atlanta is open to the public.

Tours of the Birth Home Begin Every Half-Hour At Visitor Information Station ←522 Auburn Ave. N.E.

Birth Home Of Martin L. King, Jr.

The boyhood home of Martin Luther King, Jr.

M.L.'s father was a minister at Ebenezer Baptist Church in Atlanta, Georgia.

M.L.'s father was the minister of a church. He taught his children to stand up for what is right. He taught them to speak out against what is wrong. He taught them that all people deserve justice, which means that they should be treated fairly.

When he was six, M.L.'s best friend told him he was no longer allowed to play with M.L. Why? Because M.L. was black and his friend was white.

Segregation (SEG-rih-GAY-shun) laws were meant to keep black people and white people apart. They kept kids apart, too. M.L. felt bad. Why wasn't he good enough to play with his friend?

Words to Know

SEGREGATION: Keeping someone or something apart from others

This movie theater had a separate rear entrance for blacks.

M.L.'s mother told him he was just as good as anybody else. And she told him the world was wrong. He wiped his tears. Then M.L. promised that one day he would change the world.

Father

Mother

Grandmother

M.L.

Brother Alfred Daniel

Sister Christine

M.L.'s family

Change for Peace

Martin Luther King, Jr., received the Nobel Peace Prize in 1964. At that time, he was the youngest person ever to have received it. He was just 35 years old.

Nobel Peace Prize medal

Words to Know

NOBEL PEACE PRIZE: An important award given for outstanding work toward peace

In His Time

Martin Luther King, Jr., was a boy in the late 1930s. Many things were different from how they are today.

Transportation

Most people still traveled by horse and buggy. Only some people were lucky enough to have cars.

Cities

Some of New York City's famous skyscrapers were finished in the 1930s. Two of them are the Empire State Building (left) and Rockefeller Center.

Money

Candy bars cost about a penny. That doesn't sound like much, but dollars and pennies were worth a lot more back then.

U.S. Events

Many people did not have jobs during this time, called the Great Depression. Most people had very little money.

Toys and Free Time

Children played board games and listened to programs on the radio for fun.

School

Times were tough. Some families couldn't afford to send their kids to school. Books, clothes, and shoes were too expensive.

A Way With Words

M.L. grew up listening to sermons in church. He learned how powerful words can be used to help people understand ideas.

When M.L. was 14, he entered a speech contest. He put his anger about the unfairness of separate rules for white people and black people into words. He made people think. He made them feel. The judges loved his speech, and he won.

In His Own Words

". . . let us see to it that . . . we give fair play and free opportunity for all people."

—*from M.L.'s winning speech when he was 14 years old*

Ebenezer Baptist Church is where M.L. learned the power of words.

M.L. not only grew up in Ebenezer Baptist Church, but he later became a minister there as well.

Words to Know

SERMON: A long talk, usually given in church

White passengers could sit in the front of the bus.
Black passengers had to sit in the back or stand.

On the bus ride home from the speech contest, the driver told M.L. and his teacher to give up their seats to white people. M.L. had to stand for two hours. He was mad. But he didn't say anything. He knew he could be arrested, hurt, or even killed if he did.

NOTICE

IT IS REQUIRED BY LAW. UNDER PENALTY OF FINE OF $5.00 TO $25.00 THAT WHITE AND NEGRO PASSENGERS MUST OCCUPY THE RESPECTIVE SPACE OR SEATS INDICATED BY SIGNS IN THIS VEHICLE.

TEXAS PENAL CODE: ARTICLE 1659. SEC. 4
DALLAS CITY ORDINANCE: NO. 2904

A man attaches a segregated seating sign to a bus in the southern U.S.

A Student of Peace

M.L. (third from the left) with fellow students at Morehouse College

That's a Fact!

M.L. skipped two grades in high school. He started college very early—at age 15.

M.L. worked hard in school. He finished college when he was 19 years old. He moved to the northeastern U.S. and continued in school. He wanted to be a minister like his father.

Morehouse College

In 1952, M.L. met Coretta Scott and fell in love. They got married and moved south to Alabama. There, M.L. worked as a minister. By 1955, he had gone as far as you can go in school. He had earned the title "doctor." Now he was "Dr. King."

Dexter Avenue Baptist Church in Montgomery, Alabama, where Dr. King was minister

Dr. Martin Luther King, Jr., and Coretta Scott King in 1956

Helping Others

A white man and a black man drink at separate drinking fountains.

The Kings moved back to the South to work for equal rights. They saw that not much had changed for black people there. They still couldn't swim in pools or go to school with whites. They still had to stand on buses so white people could sit.

In Alabama, Dr. King had a chance to help. A bus driver told a woman named Rosa Parks to give up her seat to a white person. But she didn't get up. Rosa Parks was arrested because she had broken the law.

Rosa Parks

The bus stop where Rosa Parks waited in 1955

Lots of people went to a meeting to decide what to do. Maids, janitors, and other working people rode the buses. They asked people not to ride buses until blacks and whites had the same rules. They called it a boycott. They put Dr. King in charge because he had a way with words.

In His Own Words

"Always feel that you count. Always feel that you have worth . . ."

Words to Know

BOYCOTT: To stop using a service as a way to protest it

For more than a year, black people walked. They took cabs. They even rode mules to get around. The boycott was not easy. But finally, people listened. Black people and white people would have the same rules on buses. Unfortunately, many white people did not follow the new rules.

People boycotting the buses wave to an empty bus driving by.

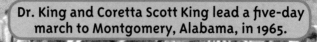

Dr. King and Coretta Scott King lead a five-day march to Montgomery, Alabama, in 1965.

In His Own Words

"Injustice anywhere is a threat to justice everywhere."

Dr. King went all over the country giving speeches. He talked about injustice and civil rights. He made people think. He made people feel. And he asked people to join him in protests for change.

Blacks and whites marched together to protest bad laws. They went to places where only whites were allowed. A lot of them got arrested. Angry people called them names. Sometimes the marchers were hurt or even killed.

Words to Know

INJUSTICE: Behavior or treatment that is unfair

LET'S BE JUST for a CHANGE No Traditions attached

Newspapers, television, and radio reported it all. People around the country were mad. They saw how bad it was to have separate rules.

Peaceful Protests

Dr. King wanted to make the world a better place. He did this with peace, not hate or violence.

People sometimes hurt him. But Dr. King did not hurt them back. He fought back with peaceful protests and powerful words.

In His Own Words

"... love is the most durable power in the world."

One person who saw what was going on was President John F. Kennedy. The President wanted to show that he agreed that rules should be the same for blacks and whites. So he invited Dr. King to visit him at the White House.

Words to Know

PEACEFUL: Quiet and not disturbed by fighting or arguing

VIOLENCE: Hurting someone or something

Dr. King

President Kennedy

President John F. Kennedy met with Dr. King and other civil rights leaders at the White House.

8 Awesome Facts About Dr. King

1

Dr. King and his father were both named Michael King. But his father changed their names in 1934.

2

Once Dr. King was hit with a brick during a peaceful march. He didn't fight back. He kept walking.

3

Dr. King liked to dance.

4

Dr. King learned good ideas from a man from India named Gandhi (GHAN-dee). He used peaceful protest to fight unfair laws.

5

Dr. King gave 2,500 speeches during the last 11 years of his life.

6

The statue of Dr. King at his memorial in Washington, D.C., is huge. Its head weighs 27 tons.

7

Dr. King told people to love each other like brothers and sisters.

8

Dr. King and Coretta Scott King had four children: Yolanda, Martin Luther III, Dexter, and Bernice.

Dr. King's Dream

That's a Fact! A draft of Dr. King's "I Have a Dream" speech is still located at Morehouse College.

Thousands of people gathered for the March on Washington in 1963.

It was August 28, 1963, in Washington, D.C. In the same city where our country makes its laws, a huge crowd of people—black and white— cheered. They had come to stand with Dr. King and protest bad laws. Everyone in the crowd wanted the same rules for white people and black people.

Dr. King's voice boomed as he gave his most famous speech, called "I Have a Dream." Dr. King's dream was for all people to be treated the same.

Hard Times

Three months after Dr. King's speech, President Kennedy was assassinated. It was a hard time for the United States. But the next President, Lyndon Johnson, kept working to change the rules.

President Johnson and Dr. King shaking hands

Words to Know

ASSASSINATE: To murder an important person

In His Own Words

"I have a dream that my four little children will one day live in a nation where they will not be judged by the color of their skin, but by the content of their character."

Dr. King speaks at the Lincoln Memorial.

His Final Years

The rules did change in 1964 and again in 1965. Laws were now the same for black people and white people. But not everyone followed the new rules right away. For the next several years, Dr. King and many others kept working. Dr. King gave speeches. He planned peaceful protests. He helped others.

In 1966, Dr. King walked black children to Mississippi schools that used to be all-white.

In 1968, Dr. King was in Memphis, Tennessee. He was helping black garbage collectors protest for better pay. But angry people still did not want change. A man with a gun assassinated Dr. King.

Black and white people around the world were very sad. They had lost a man who made them think and feel. They had lost a man who helped make our world a better place with peace and justice. But Dr. King left us his words to remember him by.

1929
Born in Atlanta, Georgia, on January 15

1948
Graduates from college; becomes a minister

1952
Met Coretta Scott. They were married a year later.

1954
Starts work at Dexter Avenue Baptist Church in Montgomery, Alabama

Dr. King's dream lives on today.

1962

Visits the
White House

1963

Arrested at a
peaceful protest
and jailed for
two weeks

1963

Speaks at
the March on
Washington

A Memorial to Peace

You can visit a national memorial to Dr. King. It is in Washington, D.C. There you can read his words about his hope that people could live together peacefully and with justice. You can also stand next to a 30-foot statue of him. It is called the "Stone of Hope."

From far away, the "Stone of Hope" looks gray. But up close, it is really many colors. The colors stand for all the different people in the world. That's because Dr. King stood up for our right to all be treated fairly.

1964
Arrested and jailed for demanding to eat at a white-only restaurant

1964
Awarded the Nobel Peace Prize

1965
Leads 25,000 people in a march to protest unfair voting laws

The "Stone of Hope" is carved out of granite. This color rock is called "Shrimp Pink."

Words to Know

MEMORIAL: Something created to remind people of a person, event, or important idea

1968

Killed on April 4 in Memphis, Tennessee

1983

A new national holiday honors Dr. King on his birthday.

2011

National memorial to Dr. King in Washington, D.C., opens.

Be a Quiz Whiz!

See how many questions you can get right! **Answers are at the bottom of page 45.**

Dr. King won a speech contest when he was:
A. 14
B. 18
C. 24
D. 9

Dr. King gave his "I Have a Dream" speech in:
A. Atlanta, Georgia
B. Washington, D.C.
C. Memphis, Tennessee
D. Boston, Massachusetts

When he was 19, Martin Luther King, Jr.:
A. Started college
B. Graduated from college
C. Got married
D. Moved to Montgomery, Alabama

4

When he was a child, Dr. King could no longer play with his best friend because:

A. He was black and his friend was white

B. He wouldn't share

C. He was poor

D. He played too rough

5

Dr. King's family nicknamed him:

A. Marty

B. Smarty

C. M.L.

D. Doc

6

The day he was killed, Dr. King was in Memphis, Tennessee, to:

A. Visit family

B. Help garbage collectors

C. Sightsee

D. Teach

7

The "Stone of Hope" is carved from granite called:

A. Dark Gray

B. Peaches-n-Cream

C. Kingstone

D. Shrimp Pink

Answers: 1) A, 2) B, 3) B, 4) A, 5) C, 6) B, 7) D

Glossary

ASSASSINATE: To murder an important person

INJUSTICE: Behavior or treatment that is unfair

MEMORIAL: Something created to remind people of a person, event, or important idea

PROTEST: To say you don't agree with something

SERMON: A long talk, usually given in church

BOYCOTT: To stop using a service as a way to protest it

CIVIL RIGHTS: The rights that all people in the U.S. have to be treated as equals

NOBEL PEACE PRIZE: An important award given for outstanding work toward peace

PEACEFUL: Quiet and not disturbed by fighting or arguing

SEGREGATION: Keeping someone or something apart from others

VIOLENCE: Hurting someone or something

Index

Bold page numbers indicate illustrations.